I0436521

FROM THE DESK OF:
SARA BELLUM

HI, SARA BELLUM HERE.

NIDA (aka the National Institute on Drug Abuse) has a blog for teens that is named after moi. NIDA is the leading research institute on drugs and drug abuse, so they are pretty much the experts on the topic (check out **www.teens.drugabuse.gov**). I'll be your "guide" for this booklet, so **READ ON...**

Is marijuana ADDICTIVE?

Yes. The chances of becoming addicted to marijuana or any drug are different for each person. For marijuana, around **1 in 11** people who use it become addicted. Could **you** be *that* one?

From age 13 to 18, **Alby** got high several times a day to help him cope. He went to school high and eventually dropped out. "I was losing focus. My attention went from 100 to zero. I was depressed," he says. Now, after getting substance abuse treatment, Alby has been able to face his problems by talking them out with counselors and making new friends he describes as "positive." As he puts it, "I feel a lot better about myself. I feel a lot sharper. I don't feel lazy anymore."

FACT

MARIJUANA—
YOU CAN GET ADDICTED.

QUIZ

Marijuana can affect learning and memory by acting in which part of the brain?

A. Hippocampus
B. Brain stem
C. Visual cortex
D. All of the above

Which of these webs is made by a spider that is NOT on drugs?

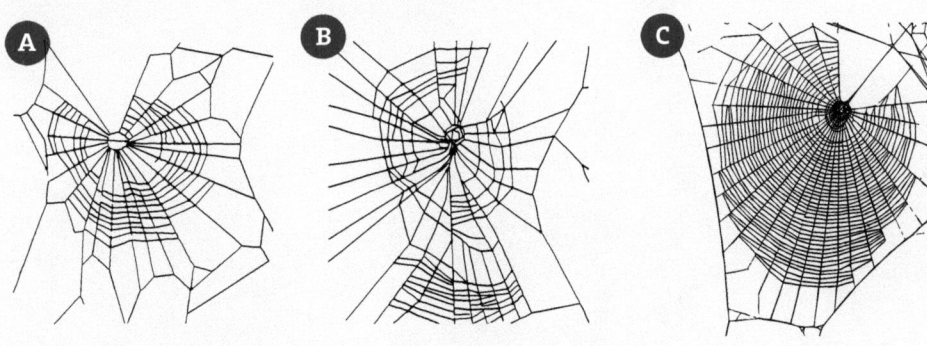

"Spice" (also known as K-2):

A. Is considered to be a "fake marijuana"
B. Has put people in emergency rooms with vomiting, confusion, and hallucinations
C. Is abused mainly by smoking
D. All of the above

Product
Placement

Product
Placement

A lot of teens ask us about **peer pressure**, or why people do things that can hurt them just to fit in.

Why do people

SMOKE

when they know it's so bad for them?

Maybe they smoke because they can't stop. People start smoking for different reasons, but most keep doing it because of one reason—they are addicted to nicotine.

DID YOU KNOW? Research says that teens who see a lot of smoking in movies are more likely to start smoking themselves. Sometimes characters smoke to look edgy and rebellious; but sometimes it's just about "product placement" — the tobacco industry trying to get into your head and your pockets.

* Product Placement

FACT

MOST PEOPLE WHO START SMOKING IN THEIR TEENS BECOME REGULAR SMOKERS BEFORE THEY'RE 18.

QUIZ

Smokeless tobacco does not cause cancer.

A. True, it is the tar in cigarettes that causes lung cancer, emphysema, and bronchial disorders.

B. False, smokeless tobacco (such as chewing tobacco and snuff) increases the risk of cancer, especially oral cancers.

How many Americans die from diseases associated with tobacco use each year?

A. About 1,500

B. About 13,200

C. About 50,500

D. About 440,000

DRINKING

and driving can add up to tragic endings. In the U.S., about 5,000 people under age 21 die each year from injuries caused by underage drinking, nearly 40 percent (1,900) in car crashes.

FACT

More than 4 in 10 people who begin drinking before age 15 eventually become alcoholics.

HIV

Getting HIV from unprotected sex

When you can't think straight because you're drunk or high, you may forget to play it safe. Kim did—read her story at:

www.hiv.drugabuse.gov/english/ webisodes/theParty.html

Meth

Meth reduces the amount of protective saliva around the teeth. People who use meth also tend to drink a lot of sugary soda, neglect personal hygiene, grind their teeth, and clench their jaws—all of which can cause what's known as "meth mouth."

Meth users sometimes hallucinate that insects are creeping on top of or underneath their skin (called formication). The person will pick or scratch their skin, trying to get rid of the imaginary "crank bugs"...soon their face and arms are covered with open sores that can get infected. See more at my blog: **www.teens.drugabuse.gov/blog**

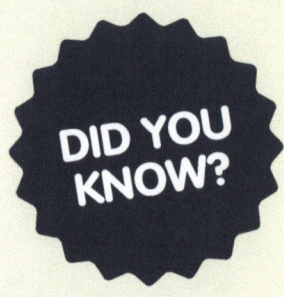

You are getting bombarded with messages about drugs in songs and movies. A study of the most popular songs in 2005 found that about:

songs said something about drug, alcohol, or tobacco use.

rap songs said something about drug, alcohol, or tobacco use.

And of the top 90 movies over the last two decades, almost

movies showed characters smoking.

movies showed people getting drunk.

Get the facts, and make your own decisions.

Tobacco

Wrinkles, bad breath, yellow teeth, wheezing, stinky clothes?...Let me at those cigarettes!

ADDICTION

SKIN DAMAGE

CATARACTS

WRINKLES

MOUTH CANCERS

THROAT CANCER

HEART DISEASE

LUNG DISEASE

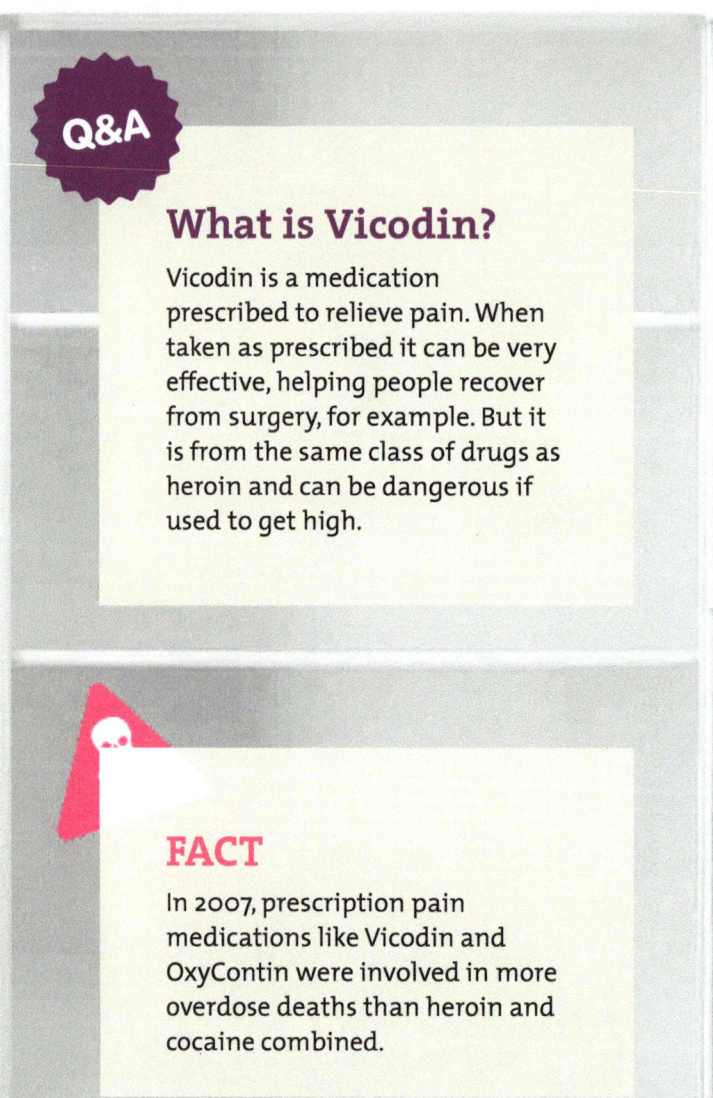

Q&A

What is Vicodin?

Vicodin is a medication prescribed to relieve pain. When taken as prescribed it can be very effective, helping people recover from surgery, for example. But it is from the same class of drugs as heroin and can be dangerous if used to get high.

FACT

In 2007, prescription pain medications like Vicodin and OxyContin were involved in more overdose deaths than heroin and cocaine combined.

A lot of you have asked: how can

PRESCRIPTION DRUGS

be harmful when they're prescribed by doctors?

Prescription drugs aren't bad—they totally help a lot of people. It really depends on the *who*, *how*, and *why* of it—*who* were they prescribed for (you or someone else?), *how* are you taking them (as prescribed or not?), and *why* (to get well or to get high)?

Some teens abuse stimulants thinking it will improve their grades; in fact, it may do just the opposite!

FACT

RX DRUG ABUSE IS DRUG ABUSE.

QUIZ

It's safe to use prescription medications when:

A. You've checked out WebMD and know what you are doing.
B. You've taken them before for another problem.
C. They are prescribed for you by a doctor for a current problem.
D. Your mom gave them to you from her prescription.
E. All of the above.

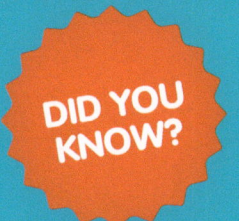

DID YOU KNOW?

Mixing pills with other drugs or with alcohol really increases your risk of death from accidental overdose.

Abuse of prescription stimulants like Ritalin and Adderall can cause serious health problems, including panic attacks, seizures, and heart attacks.

ANSWERS: C. They are prescribed for you by a doctor for a current problem.

21

You know they make you

FUZZY,

but what do drugs do to your brain?

Different drugs do different things. But they *all* affect the brain—that's why drugs make you feel high, low, speeded up, slowed down, or see things that aren't there.

DID YOU KNOW? Repeated drug use can reset the brain's pleasure meter, so that without the drug, you feel hopeless and sad. Eventually, everyday fun stuff like spending time with friends or playing with your dog doesn't make you happy anymore.

Justin posted a comment on my blog saying he always thought that if he "huffs" markers in small doses, just every once in a while, it will cause little or no damage to his brain cells. Maybe, maybe not. We're all different, so you never know when something dangerous will happen to you. Huffing may make you high for a few minutes, but it can damage your brain for a whole lot longer.

FACT

DRUGS MESS WITH YOUR BRAIN'S WIRING AND SIGNALS.

QUIZ

Some drugs affect the brain because their chemical structures are similar to natural brain chemicals called:

    A. neurons

    B. axons

    C. neurotransmitters

    D. dendrites

Sniffing markers can harm the brain by affecting a fatty tissue called:

    A. myelin

    B. noradrenaline

    C. frontal cortex

    D. polyneuropathy

Salvia is a herb that can make you:

    A. Feel a surge of connectedness to what's around you.

    B. Experience hallucinations and emotional swings.

    C. Feel detached and less able to interact with what's going on.

    D. Both b and c.

    E. Both a and b.

REHAB?

Does treatment really work—why do people come and go so much?

It takes time to recover from addiction—not only for the brain to re-adjust, but to make lifestyle changes to avoid drugs. Think how hard it is for people trying to lose weight—they try different diets, exercise for a while, lose a few pounds only to gain them back... until they can make lasting changes to keep the weight off. Same with quitting drugs—it may take several rounds of treatment before it sticks.

DID YOU KNOW?

1-800-662-HELP

Different types of treatments are available to meet your specific needs. You can get referrals to treatment programs by calling 1-800-662-HELP (a confidential hotline), or by visiting the Substance Abuse and Mental Health Services Administration on line at **www.findtreatment. samhsa.gov**.

FACT

THERE IS TREATMENT AND IT WORKS.

QUIZ

A person who is addicted to drugs...

A. Is beyond reach.
B. Can be helped with treatment.
C. Needs a brain transplant.
D. Can easily quit if they want to.

What do YOU think?

We know you have a lot of questions about drugs. We do too, and we'd love to hear from you! So go to my blog at **http://teens. drugabuse.gov/blog/what-do-you-think/** and let us know what you think about the questions below—and thanks for sharing!

1. How do you convince a friend who is using drugs that they may be at risk for addiction or other bad consequences even though they feel fine right now?

2. Knowing what we do now, would you make cigarettes illegal if you could?

3. What is the best way to convince you or your friends that prescription drugs can be dangerous when abused— without scaring the people who need them?

4. Do you consider it cheating when athletes use steroids to improve their performance—what should the consequences be?

5. What's the best way to get messages out to teens—social networks, TV ads, Web sites? Who should the messages be from?

If we haven't covered something you want to know about, go to **www.teens.drugabuse.gov** and enter your topic in the search box.

www.ingramcontent.com/pod-product-compliance
Lightning Source LLC
Chambersburg PA
CBHW060810290526
45792CB00005BA/1598